# God's Little Instruction Book for Students

A Collection of Simple, Humorous, and Motivational Sayings to Inspire You to Greatness!

Honor Books, Inc. • P.O. Box 55388 • Tulsa, OK 74155

*God's Little Instruction Book for Students*
ISBN 1-56292-057-X
Copyright © 1994 by Honor Books, Inc.
P.O. Box 55388
Tulsa, Oklahoma 74155

# INTRODUCTION

*God's Little Instruction Book for Students* is an inspirational collection of quotes and Scriptures that will motivate students in high school and college to live a meaningful, productive and happy life while inspiring them to strive for excellence and character in living.

This delightful book is basic, practical and filled with the timeless wisdom of the Bible, covering topics that students everywhere can appreciate and learn more about. *God's Little Instruction Book for Students* will help students reach for excellence as they meet the challenges of the future.

# Acknowledgments

We acknowledge and thank the following people for the quotes used in this book: Syrus (6), Dr. Eugene Swearingen (8,19,30), Gary Smalley and John Treat (9,148), Calvin Coolidge (11,106), Andre Maurois (12), David Shibley (13), Bill Copeland (14), Harry Emerson Fosdick (15,103), John D. Rockefeller, Jr. (16), Les Brown (17), Thomas Jefferson (18,59), Robert C. Edward (20), Ed Cole (21,33,141), Benjamin Franklin (22,113), Kin Hubbard (25), Henry Ward Beecher (26), John A. Shedd (28), Dwight L. Moody (31,45), H. E. Jansen (34), A. W. Tozer (38), Roy Disney (39), Bob Bales (40), Helen Keller (41), Seneca (42), Aristotle (43,82,134), Matthew Prior (44), William A. Ward (46), Katherine Graham (47), Moliere (49), Descartes (50), Solon (51), Charles C. Noble (52), Samuel Johnson (53), Eleanor Roosevelt (54), John Sculley (55), George Bernard Shaw (56), Henry Wadsworth Longfellow (57), Ralph Waldo Emerson (61,81), Oprah Winfrey (62), Charles H. Spurgeon (63), William Lyon Phelps (64), Franklin (65), Terence (67), Pauline H. Peters (73), Josh Billings (74), Andrew Jackson (75), Jean Paul Richter (76), William James (77), Samuel Butler (78), H. P. Liddon (79), George Elliot (80), John R. Rice (83), William H. Danforth (84,94,122), Thomas A. Edison (85), Orlando Battista (86,102), George Edward Woodberry (87), Ronald E. Osborn (88), Woodrow Wilson (89), Winston Churchill (90,133), Washington Irving (91), Thomas Carlyle (92), Lillian Dickson (95), Denis Diserot (96), Earl Nightingale (97,126), Horace (98), Louis D. Brandeis (99), Hannah More (100), Publilius Syrus (101), Victor Hugo (104), David Dunn (105), Mark Twain (107,140), Roy L. Smith (108), Phil Marquart (109), Oliver Wendell Holmes (110), James Whitcomb Riley (111), George Washington (112), Jeremy Taylor (116), Say (117), Cervantes (118), Bacon (121), Zig Ziglar (123,129), H. W. Beecher (124), Builder (125), Abraham Lincoln (127), Diane Sawyer (130), Wilson Mizner (131), Beverly Sills (132), Winifred Newman (135), Mike Murdock (136), Witt Fowler (137), Theodore Roosevelt (138), Leo Tolstoy (139), Henry Ford (142), Bill Cosby (143), George Dana Boardman (144), Vince Lombardi (145), George Sala (146), Samuel Johnson (147)

When you were born, you cried and the world rejoiced. Live your life in such a manner that when you die the world cries and you rejoice.

*The memory of the righteous will be a blessing....*
Proverbs 10:7 NIV

# Many receive advice, only the wise profit by it.

*Pride only breeds quarrels, but wisdom
is found in those who take advice.*
Proverbs 13:10 NIV

# Even a mosquito doesn't get a slap on the back until it starts to work.

*Work hard so God can say to you, "Well done." Be a good workman, one who does not need to be ashamed when God examines your work....*
2 Timothy 2:15 TLB

# You will never make a more important decision than the person you marry.

*Therefore shall a man leave his father and his mother,*
*and shall cleave unto his wife: and they shall be one flesh.*
Genesis 2:24

# The Bible has a word to describe "safe" sex: It's called marriage.

*Marriage should be honored by all, and the marriage bed kept pure, for God will judge the adulterer and all the sexually immoral.*
Hebrews 13:4 NIV

# We too often love things and use people, when we should be using things and loving people.

*Be devoted to one another in brotherly love.*
*Honor one another above yourselves.*
Romans 12:10 NIV

# I have never been hurt by anything I didn't say.

*Don't talk so much. You keep putting your foot in your mouth.*
*Be sensible and turn off the flow!*
Proverbs 10:19 TLB

The greedy search for money
or success will almost always lead
men into unhappiness. Why? Because
that kind of life makes them depend
upon things outside themselves.

*Let your character be free from the love of money,*
*being content with what you have; for He Himself has said,*
*"I will never desert you nor will I ever forsake you."*
Hebrews 13:5 NAS

One hundred years from now it won't matter if you got that big break, took the trip to Europe, or finally traded up to a Mercedes.... It will greatly matter, one hundred years from now, that you made a commitment to Jesus Christ.

*For what is a man profited, if he shall gain the whole world, and lose his own soul?....*
Matthew 16:26

# Success is knowing the difference between cornering people and getting them in your corner.

*Can two walk together, except they be agreed?*
Amos 3:3

# No horse gets anywhere until he is harnessed. No life ever grows great until it is focused, dedicated, disciplined.

*In a race, everyone runs but only one person gets first prize...
to win the contest you must deny yourselves many
things that would keep you from doing your best.*
1 Corinthians 9:24a,25 TLB

# The secret of success is to do the common things uncommonly well.

*Seest thou a man diligent in his business? he shall stand before kings; he shall not stand before mean men.*
Proverbs 22:29

# Shoot for the moon. Even if you miss it you will land among the stars.

*Aim for perfection....*
2 Corinthians 13:11b NIV

# I like the dreams of the future better than the history of the past.

*Remember ye not the former things, neither consider the things of old. Behold, I will do a new thing....*
Isaiah 43:18,19

# The way to get to the top is to get off your bottom.

*How long will you lie down, O sluggard?*
*When will you arise from your sleep?*
Proverbs 6:9 NAS

# You are only what you are when no one is looking.

*Not with eyeservice, as menpleasers; but as the servants of Christ, doing the will of God from the heart.*
Ephesians 6:6

# There are times when silence is golden, other times it is just plain yellow.

*To everything there is a season....: a time to keep silence, and a time to speak.*
Ecclesiastes 3:1,7b

# Keep thy shop and thy shop will keep thee.

*He who works his land will have abundant food,*
*but he who chases fantasies lacks judgement.*
Proverbs 12:11 NIV

# Every job is a self-portrait of the person who does it. Autograph your work with excellence.

*Daniel was preferred above the presidents and princes,*
*because an excellent spirit was in him....*
Daniel 6:3

# The best things in life are *not* free.

*Forasmuch as ye know that ye were not redeemed with corruptible things, as silver and gold...but with the precious blood of Christ, as of a lamb without blemish and without spot.*
1 Peter 1:18,19

# You can lead a boy to college, but you cannot make him think.

*It is senseless to pay tuition to educate
a rebel who has no heart for truth.*
Proverbs 17:16 TLB

# If a man cannot be a Christian in the place where he is, he cannot be a Christian anywhere.

*Don't work hard only when your master is watching and then shirk when he isn't looking; work hard and with gladness all the time, as though working for Christ, doing the will of God with all your hearts.*
Ephesians 6:6,7 TLB

# Don't ask God for what you think is good; ask Him for what He thinks is good for you.

*After this manner therefore pray ye.... Thy kingdom come.
Thy will be done in earth, as it is in heaven.*
Matthew 6:9,10

# Opportunities are seldom labeled.

*...seek, and ye shall find; knock,*
*and it shall be opened unto you.*
Matthew 7:7

# The wise does at once what the fool does at last.

*He that gathereth in summer is a wise son:*
*but he that sleepeth in harvest is a son that causeth shame.*
Proverbs 10:5

# Definition of status: Buying something you don't need with money you don't have to impress people you don't like.

*But they do all their deeds to be noticed by men....*
Matthew 23:5 NAS

Trust in yourself and you are doomed to disappointment;...but trust in God, and you are never to be confounded in time or eternity.

*It is better to take refuge in the Lord than to trust in man.*
Psalm 118:8 NIV

# Don't be discouraged; everyone who got where he is, started where he was.

*Though your beginning was insignificant,*
*Yet your end will increase greatly.*
Job 8:7 NAS

# Maturity doesn't come with age; it comes with acceptance of responsibility.

*When I was a child, I spake as a child, I understood as a child, I thought as a child; but when I became a man, I put away childish things.*
1 Corinthians 13:11

# The man who wins may have been counted out several times, but he didn't hear the referee.

*For though a righteous man falls seven times, he rises again....*
Proverbs 24:16 NIV

# The happiest people don't necessarily have the best of everything. They just make the best of everything.

*...For I have learned, in whatsoever state I am, therewith to be content.*
*I can do all things through Christ which strengtheneth me.*
Philippians 4:11,13

# Keep company with good men and good men you will imitate.

*Iron sharpeneth iron; so a man sharpeneth
the countenance of his friend.*
Proverbs 27:17

# Learn by experience — preferably other people's.

*All these things happened to them as examples —*
*as object lessons to us — to warn us against doing the same things....*
1 Corinthians 10:11 TLB

It is not what a man
does that determines
whether his work
is sacred or secular,
it is why he does it.

*Whatever you do, work at it with all your heart, as working
for the Lord, not for men.... It is the Lord Christ you are serving.*
Colossians 3:23,24 NIV

# It's not hard to make decisions when you know what your values are.

*But Daniel purposed in his heart that he would not defile himself....*
Daniel 1:8

Don't cross your bridges until you get to them. We spend our lives defeating ourselves crossing bridges we never get to.

*So, don't be anxious about tomorrow. God will take care of your tomorrow too. Live one day at a time.*
Matthew 6:34 TLB

I am only one; but still
I am one. I cannot do
everything, but still I
can do something; I
will not refuse to do
the something I can do.

*Under his (Christ's) direction the whole body is fitted together perfectly,*
*and each part in its own special way helps the other parts....*
Ephesians 4:16 TLB

# Politeness goes far, yet costs nothing.

*A kind man benefits himself....*
Proverbs 11:17 NIV

We should behave
to our friends as we
would wish our friends
to behave to us.

*And as ye would that men should do to you,*
*do ye also to them likewise.*
Luke 6:31

# The end must justify the means.

*The just man walketh in his integrity:*
*his children are blessed after him.*
Proverbs 20:7

# Character is what you are in the dark.

*The integrity of the upright shall guide them....*
Proverbs 11:3

# Adversity causes some men to break; others to break records.

*If thou faint in the day of adversity, thy strength is small.*
Proverbs 24:10

# To love what you do and feel that it matters — how could anything be more fun?

*...for my heart rejoiced in all my labour....*
Ecclesiastes 2:10

# A man who wants to lead the orchestra must turn his back on the crowd.

*Wherefore come out from among them, and be ye separate, saith the
Lord, and touch not the unclean thing; and I will receive you.*
2 Corinthians 6:17

# Men are alike in their promises. It is only in their deeds that they differ.

*Many a man claims to have unfailing love,*
*but a faithful man who can find?*
Proverbs 20:6 NIV

# Conquer yourself rather than the world.

*Similarly, encourage the young men to be self-controlled.*
Titus 2:6 NIV

# He that has learned to obey will know how to command.

*The wise in heart accept commands,*
*but a chattering fool comes to ruin.*
Proverbs 10:8 NIV

# You must have long-range goals to keep you from being frustrated by short-range failures.

*Let us fix our eyes on Jesus, the author and perfecter of our faith,
who for the joy set before him endured the cross, scorning its shame,
and sat down at the right hand of the throne of God.*
Hebrews 9:27

# Clear your mind of can't.

*I can do all things through Christ which strengtheneth me.*
Philippians 4:13

# The future belongs to those who believe in the beauty of their dreams.

*...anything is possible if you have faith.*
Mark 9:23 TLB

# The future belongs to those who see possibilities before they become obvious.

*For the vision is yet for an appointed time...*
*it will surely come, it will not tarry.*
Habakkuk 2:3

When I was a young man
I observed that nine out
of ten things I did were
failures. I didn't want
to be a failure, so I did
ten times more work.

*He becometh poor that dealeth with a slack hand:*
*but the hand of the diligent maketh rich.*
Proverbs 10:4

Perseverance is a great
element of success;
if you only knock long
enough and loud enough
at the gate you are sure
to wake up somebody.

*...Ask, and it shall be given you; seek, and ye shall find;
knock, and it shall be opened unto you.*
Luke 11:9

# Jumping to conclusions is not half as good an exercise as digging for facts.

*Study to show thyself approved unto God, a workman that needeth not to be ashamed, rightly dividing the word of truth.*
2 Timothy 2:15

The most valuable of all talents is that of never using two words when one will do.

*In the multitude of words there wanteth not sin:*
*but he that refraineth his lips is wise.*
Proverbs 10:19

# Laziness is often mistaken for patience.

*...let us lay aside every weight, and the sin which doth so easily beset us, and let us run with patience the race that is set before us.*
Hebrews 12:1

# Nothing great was ever achieved without enthusiasm.

*...for the joy of the Lord is your strength.*
Nehemiah 8:10

# Luck is a matter of preparation meeting opportunity.

*...make the most of every opportunity.*
Colossians 4:5 NIV

# Carve your name on hearts and not on marble.

*The only letter I need is you yourselves! They can see that you are a letter from Christ written by us....not one carved on stone, but in human hearts.*
2 Corinthians 3:2a,3 TLB

# A knowledge of the Bible without a college course is more valuable than a college course without the Bible.

*All scripture is given by inspiration of God, and is profitable for doctrine, for reproof, for correction, for instruction in righteousness: that the man of God may be perfect, thoroughly furnished unto all good works.*
2 Timothy 3:16,17

One-half the trouble
of this life can be
traced to saying yes
too quick, and not
saying no soon enough.

*Seest thou a man that is hasty in his words?*
*there is more hope of a fool than of him.*
Proverbs 29:20

# There is no poverty that can overtake diligence.

*He becometh poor that dealeth with a slack hand:*
*but the hand of the diligent maketh rich.*
Proverbs 10:4

# Never despair; but if you do, work on in despair.

*But as for you, be strong and do not give up,*
*for your work will be rewarded.*
2 Chronicles 15:7 NIV

You can accomplish more
in one hour with God than
one lifetime without Him.

*...with God all things are possible.*
Matthew 19:26

# If you don't stand for something you'll fall for anything!

*...If you do not stand firm in your faith,*
*you will not stand at all.*
Isaiah 7:9 NIV

# The difference between ordinary and extraordinary is that little extra.

*Whatsoever thy hand findeth to do, do it with thy might....*
Ecclesiastes 9:10

Man cannot discover
new oceans unless he
has the courage to lose
sight of the shore.

*...and Peter got out of the boat, and walked*
*on the water and came toward Jesus.*
Matthew 14:29 NAS

Every man is enthusiastic at times.
One man has enthusiasm for thirty
minutes, another has it for thirty days —
but it is the man that has it for thirty
years who makes a success in life.

*...let us run with perseverance the race marked out for us.*
Hebrews 12:1 NIV

## "The Supervisor's Prayer"

Lord when I am wrong, make me willing to change; when I am right, make, me easy to live with. So strengthen me that the power of my example will far exceed the authority of my rank.

*...to offer ourselves as a model for you,*
*that you might follow our example.*
2 Thessalonians 3:9 NAS

Consider the postage
stamp: its usefulness
consists in the ability
to stick to one thing
till it gets there.

*I have fought a good fight, I have finished my course,*
*I have kept the faith.*
2 Timothy 4:7

# One man with courage makes a majority.

*Be strong and of good courage. . . for the Lord thy God. . .*
*will not fail thee, nor forsake thee.*
Deuteronomy 31:6

# A man never discloses his own character so clearly as when he describes another's.

*A good man out of the good treasure of the heart bringeth forth good things; and an evil man out of the evil treasure bringeth forth evil things.*
Matthew 12:35

# The greatest use of life is to spend it for something that will outlast it.

*But store up for yourselves treasures in heaven, where moth and rust do not destroy, and where thieves do not break in and steal.*
Matthew 6:20 NIV

Every man's work,
whether it be literature,
or music, or pictures,
or architecture, or
anything else, is always
a portrait of himself.

*As in water face reflects face, so the heart of man reflects man.*
Proverbs 27:19 NAS

What we do on some great occasion will probably depend on what we already are; and what we are will be the result of previous years of self-discipline.

*But I keep under my body, and bring it into subjection....*
1 Corinthians 9:27

# Our deeds determine us, as much as we determine our deeds.

*Even a child is known by his actions,*
*by whether his conduct is pure and right.*
Proverbs 20:11 NIV

# What you do speaks so loud that I cannot hear what you say.

*Show me your faith without deeds,
and I will show you my faith by what I do.*
James 2:18b NIV

# All virtue is summed up in dealing justly.

*He hath shewed thee, O man, what is good; and what doth the Lord require of thee, but to do justly, and to love mercy, and to walk humbly with thy God?*
Micah 6:8

# No matter what a man's past may have been, his future is spotless.

*...forgetting those things which are behind, and reaching forth unto those things which are before.*
Philippians 3:13

# One of life's great rules is this: The more you give, the more you get.

*The liberal soul shall be made fat: and he that watereth shall be watered also himself.*
Proverbs 11:24,25

# Everything comes to him who hustles while he waits.

*We do not want you to become lazy, but to imitate those who through faith and patience inherit what has been promised.*
Hebrews 6:12 NIV

# A well-trained memory is one that permits you to forget everything that isn't worth remembering.

*Finally, brethren, whatsoever things are true, whatsoever things are honest, whatsoever things are just...if there be any virtue, and if there be any praise, think on these things.*
Philippians 4:8

# Defeat is not the worst of failures. Not to have tried is the true failure.

*Be strong and of a good courage; be not afraid,*
*neither be thou dismayed: for the Lord thy God*
*is with thee whithersoever thou goest.*
Joshua 1:9

# Unless you try to do something beyond what you have already mastered, you will never grow.

*...reaching forth unto those things which are before, I press toward the mark for the prize of the high calling of God in Christ Jesus.*
Philippians 3:13,14

I would rather fail in
the cause that someday
will triumph than
triumph in a cause
that someday will fail.

*Now thanks be unto God, which
always causeth us to triumph in Christ....*
2 Corinthians 2:14

# Kites rise highest against the wind, not with it.

*For when the way is rough, your patience has a chance to grow.*
*So let it grow, and don't try to squirm out of your problems.*
James 1:3,4a TLB

# Little minds are tamed and subdued by misfortune; but great minds rise above them.

*For a just man falleth seven times, and riseth up again....*
Proverbs 24:16

...the cheerful man will do more in the same time, will do it better, will preserve it longer, than the sad or sullen.

*When a man is gloomy, everything seems to go wrong; when he is cheerful, everything seems right!*
Proverbs 15:15 TLB

The secret of success
is to be like a duck —
smooth and unruffled
on top, but paddling
furiously underneath.

*...but I laboured more abundantly than they all:
yet not I, but the grace of God which was with me.*
1 Corinthians 15:10

# No plan is worth the paper it is printed on unless it starts you doing something.

*But be ye doers of the word, and not hearers only,
deceiving your own selves.*
James 1:22

# Life is a coin. You can spend it any way you wish, but you can spend it only once.

*And as it is appointed unto men once to die,*
*but after this the judgment.*
Hebrews 12:2 NIV

# Only passions, great passions, can elevate the soul to great things.

*...fervent in spirit; serving the Lord.*
Romans 12:11

# Failures want pleasing methods, successes want pleasing results.

*No discipline seems pleasant at the time, but painful.*
*Later on, however, it produces a harvest of righteousness*
*and peace for those who have been trained by it.*
Hebrews 12:11 NIV

# Once a word has been allowed to escape, it cannot be recalled.

*Let no corrupt communication proceed out of your mouth,*
*but that which is good to the use of edifying,*
*that it may minister grace unto the hearers.*
Ephesians 4:29

Most of the things worth doing in the world had been declared impossible before they were done.

*...but with God all things are possible.*
Matthew 19:26

# Obstacles are those frightful things you see when you take your eyes off the goal.

*So Peter....walked on the water toward Jesus. But when he looked around at the high waves, he was terrified and began to sink....*
Matthew 14:29,30 TLB

# A good reputation is more valuable than money.

*A good name is rather to be chosen than great riches....*
Proverbs 22:1

# An error doesn't become a mistake until you refuse to correct it.

*He who heeds discipline shows the way to life,*
*but whoever ignores correction leads others astray.*
Proverbs 10:17 NIV

# Hating people is like burning down your own house to get rid of a rat.

*But if ye bite and devour one another,*
*take heed that ye be not consumed one of another.*
Galatians 5:15

# Laughter is the sun that drives winter from the human face.

*A merry heart maketh a cheerful countenance:*
*but by sorrow of the heart the spirit is broken.*
Proverbs 15:13

# Good nature begets smiles, smiles beget friends, and friends are better than a fortune.

*The light in the eyes (of him whose heart is joyful)*
*rejoices the heart of others....*
Proverbs 15:30 AMP

No person was ever
honored for what he
received. Honor has
been the reward
for what he gave.

*...the righteous give without sparing.*
Proverbs 21:26 NIV

The difference between
the right word and
the almost right word
is the difference
between lightning
and the lightning bug.

*A word fitly spoken is like apples of gold in pictures of silver.*
Proverbs 25:11

This world belongs to
the man who is wise
enough to change
his mind in the
presence of facts.

*...whoever heeds correction gains understanding.*
Proverbs 15:32 NIV

Blessed is the man who is too busy to worry in the daytime and too sleepy to worry at night.

*The sleep of a labouring man is sweet....*
Ecclesiastes 5:12

# Every calling is great when greatly pursued.

*I press toward the mark for the prize*
*of the high calling of God in Christ Jesus.*
Philippians 3:14

# The ripest peach is highest on the tree.

*Let us not become weary in doing good, for at the proper time we will reap a harvest if we do not give up.*
Galatians 6:9 NIV

# 'Tis better to be alone, than in bad company.

*Do not be misled: "Bad company corrupts good character."*
1 Corinthians 15:33 NIV

# The rotten apple spoils his companion.

*He that walketh with wise men shall be wise:*
*but a companion of fools shall be destroyed.*
Proverbs 13:20

# Patience is bitter but its fruit is sweet.

*For ye have need of patience, that, after ye have done the will of God, ye might receive the promise.*
Hebrews 10:36

# It needs more skill
## than I can tell
## To play the second
## fiddle well.

*But he that is greatest among you shall be your servant.*
Matthew 23:11

# It is impossible for that man to despair who remembers that his Helper is omnipotent.

*I will lift up my eyes to the mountains; from whence shall my help come?*
*My help comes from the Lord, who made the heaven and earth.*
Psalm 121:1,2 NAS

# School seeks to get you ready for examination; life gives the finals.

*Examine yourselves to see whether you
are in the faith; test yourselves.*
2 Corinthians 13:5 NIV

# Diligence is the mother of good fortune.

*The plans of the diligent lead to profit....*
Proverbs 21:5 NIV

# The road to success is dotted with many tempting parking places.

*...let us lay aside every weight, and the sin which doth so easily beset us, and let us run with patience the race that is set before us.*
Hebrews 12:1

# When you are laboring for others let it be with the same zeal as if it were for yourself.

*Each of you should look not only to your own interests,*
*but also to the interest of others.*
Philippians 2:4 NIV

# Money is a good servant but a bad master.

*The rich ruleth over the poor, and the borrower
is servant to the lender.*
Proverbs 22:7

Treat everybody alike, no matter from what station in life he comes. ...really great men and women are those who are natural, frank and honest with everyone with whom they come into contact.

*...don't show favoritism.*
James 2:1 NIV

When you do the things you have to do when you have to do them, the day will come when you can do the things you want to do when you want to do them.

*He becometh poor that dealeth with a slack hand:*
*but the hand of the diligent maketh rich.*
Proverbs 10:4

A man without mirth is like a wagon without springs, he is jolted disagreeably by every pebble in the road.

*A merry heart doeth good like a medicine:*
*but a broken spirit drieth the bones.*
Proverbs 17:22

The 2 most important words: "Thank you." The most important word: "We." The least important word: "I."

*Don't be selfish.... Be humble, thinking of others as better than yourself.*
Philippians 2:3 TLB

# Here's the key of success and the key to failure: we become what we think about....

*Finally, brethren, whatsoever things are true, whatsoever things are honest...if there be any virtue, and if there be any praise, think on these things.*
Philippians 4:8

Always bear in mind that your own resolution to success is more important than any other one thing.

*For the Lord God will help me; therefore shall I not be confounded: therefore have I set my face like a flint, and I know that I shall not be ashamed.*
Isaiah 50:7

# Triumph is just "umph" added to try.

*Whatsoever thy hand findeth to do, do it with thy might....*
Ecclesiastes 9:10

# A goal properly set is halfway reached.

*And the LORD answered me, and said, Write the vision,*
*and make it plain upon tables, that he may run that readeth it.*
Habakkuk 2:2

I think the one lesson
I have learned is that
there is no substitute
for paying attention.

*Therefore we ought to give the more earnest heed to the things which we have heard, lest at any time we should let them slip.*
Hebrews 2:1

# A good listener is not only popular everywhere, but after a while he knows something.

*The ear that heareth the reproof of life abideth among the wise.*
Proverbs 15:31

# You may be disappointed if you fail, but you are doomed if you don't try.

*The sluggard craves and gets nothing, but the desires of the diligent are fully satisfied.*
Proverbs 13:4 NIV

# Success is never final; failure is never fatal; it is courage that counts.

*Be of good courage, and he shall strengthen
your heart, all ye that hope in the Lord.*
Psalm 31:24

I count him braver
who overcomes his desires
than him who conquers
his enemies; for the
hardest victory is the
victory over self.

*I keep under my body; and bring it into subjection....*
1 Corinthians 9:27

Vision is the world's most desperate need. There are no hopeless situations, only people who think hopelessly.

*Where there is no vision, the people perish....*
Proverbs 29:18

Men will spend their health getting wealth; then, gladly pay all they have earned to get health back.

*For what will it profit a man if he gains
the whole world and forfeits his life....*
Matthew 16:26 AMP

Give me a task too big,
too hard for human hands,
then I shall come at length
to lean on Thee, and
leaning, find my strength.

*Trust in the Lord with all your heart and lean not
on your own understanding.*
Proverbs 3:5 NIV

The most important single ingredient in the formula of success is knowing how to get along with people.

*See that no one pays back evil for evil, but always try to do good to each other and to everyone else.*
1 Thessalonians 5:15 TLB

# Everyone thinks of changing the world, but no one thinks of changing himself.

*...unless you change and become like little children
you will never enter the kingdom of heaven.*
Matthew 18:3 NIV

# Courage is resistance to fear, mastery of fear — not absence of fear.

*Yea, though I walk through the valley of the shadow of death, I will fear no evil: for thou art with me; thy rod and thy staff they comfort me.*
Psalm 23:4

# Prayer is an invisible tool which is wielded in a visible world.

*For the weapons of our warfare are not carnal, but mighty through God to the pulling down of strong holds.*
2 Corinthians 10:4

# Money is like an arm or leg: use it or lose it.

*For to him who has will more be given...and he will have great plenty;*
*but for him who has not, even the little he has will be taken away.*
Matthew 13:12 TLB

# I don't know the secret to success but the key to failure is to try to please everyone.

*Am I now trying to win the approval of man or of God?*
Galatians 1:10a NIV

Let us not say, Every man is the architect of his own fortune; but let us say, Every man is the architect of his own character.

*...till I die I will not remove mine integrity from me.*
*My righteousness I hold fast, and will not let it go:*
*my heart shall not reproach me so long as I live.*
Job 27:5,6

The price of success is hard work, dedication to the job at hand, and determination that whether we win or lose, we have applied the best of ourselves to the task at hand.

*And whatsoever ye do, do it heartily, as to the Lord, and not unto men.*
Colossians 3:23

Not only to say the right thing in the right place, but far more difficult, to leave unsaid the wrong thing at the tempting moment.

*Self-control means controlling the tongue!*
*A quick retort can ruin everything.*
Proverbs 13:3 TLB

Those that have done
nothing in life are not
qualified to judge of
those that have done little.

*Judge not, and ye shall not be judged: condemn not,
and ye shall not be condemned....*
Luke 6:37

People, places, and things were never meant to give us life. God alone is the author of a fulfilling life.

*...I am come that they might have life, and that they might have it more abundantly.*
John 10:10

# COMMON COURTESIES
# FOR STUDENTS SECTION

*And just as you want people to treat you,*
*treat them in the same way.*
Luke 6:31 NAS

*So then, while we have opportunity,*
*let us do good to all men....*
Galatians 6:10 NIV

Always say *thank you*, *excuse me*, and *please* when you have done a favor or when you are apologizing.

*And just as you want people to treat you,*
*treat them in the same way.*
Luke 6:31 NAS

# Always knock and ask permission before entering someone's room.

*So then, while we have opportunity, let us do good to all men....*
Galatians 6:10 NIV

Don't put your feet up
on the furniture. Feet
do not enhance the look
of the desk or the table.

*And just as you want people to treat you, treat them in the same way.*
Luke 6:31 NAS

# Always RSVP promptly to every invitation you receive.

*So then, while we have opportunity, let us do good to all men....*
Galatians 6:10 NIV

# Return anything borrowed on time, and in good condition.

*And just as you want people to treat you, treat them in the same way.*
Luke 6:31 NAS

# Never cheat on your place in line.

*So then, while we have opportunity, let us do good to all men....*
Galatians 6:10 NIV

When you dial a wrong number, say, "I'm sorry, excuse me" – instead of slamming down the receiver in the other person's ear.

*And just as you want people to treat you, treat them in the same way.*
Luke 6:31 NAS

Be on time for appointments; leave on time, too, for nothing is more boring than someone who overstays his welcome.

*So then, while we have opportunity, let us do good to all men....*
Galatians 6:10 NIV

# Show respect to anyone in authority.

*And just as you want people to treat you, treat them in the same way.*
Luke 6:31 NAS

Learn how to pay compliments. Start with the members of your family, and you will find it will become easier later in life to compliment others.
It's a great asset.

*And just as you want people to treat you, treat them in the same way.*
Luke 6:31 NAS

Additional copies of this book and other titles
in the *God's Little Instruction Book* series
are available at your local bookstore.

*God's Little Instruction Book*
*God's Little Instruction Book II*
*God's Little Instruction Book for Mom*
*God's Little Instruction Book for Dad*
*God's Little Instruction Book for Graduates*
*God's Little Instruction Book — Special Gift Edition*
*God's Little Instruction Book Daily Calendar*

P. O. Box 55388
Tulsa, OK 74155